A YEAR OF SABBATHS

ALSO BY JOE FONTENOT

Life Hacking Spiritual Disciplines

Minimalist Marketing

A YEAR OF SABBATHS

52 MEDITATIONS ON THE CHRISTIAN LIFE

JOE FONTENOT

Five Round Rocks Media

2018

Printed in the United States of America. For information, address Five Round Rocks Media, LLC, 848 Matador Dr, Gretna, LA 70056.

Artwork design by Joe Fontenot, with design input from Samuel Fontenot.

First Five Round Rocks Media hardback edition: November 2018
First Five Round Rocks Media paperback edition: November 2018
ISBN 978-0-9981007-6-0 (hardback)
ISBN 978-0-9981007-5-3 (paperback)

Published by Five Round Rocks Media, LLC
www.FiveRoundRocks.com

To Granddad

▌INTRODUCTION ▪1

What's a modern Sabbath?
How to use this devotional

▌MEDITATIONS ▪7

■ CONCLUSION 119

WHAT'S A MODERN SABBATH?

After the industrial revolution—after we figured out that making six-year-olds work in dark factories for seventeen hours a day was not a good thing—we invented stuff like the forty-hour work week. And with that came the weekend. A time of rest.

Saturday became a day off. And so did Sunday. Life was good.

But this raised a new question. In our modern society, is the Sabbath still relevant? Or has it become an overflow option for the overworked? The ones who *need* it?

I argue that it's not only still relevant today—but that it's relevant for each and every one of us. But it's not because we get tired and need a break. In fact, I don't believe the Sabbath was ever about that kind of rest.

From the beginning

When God originally gave his people (the Israelites) the Sabbath, it was part of the ten commandments. At this time, the Israelites were nomadic, meaning they didn't have any long term residence where they could cultivate crops. They were instead dependent directly on God to provide every single day.

But shortly after this they would be putting down roots in Canaan, the Promised Land. And like the other people of the time, they would become an agrarian society, planting crops and raising animals. But unlike the world today, as it is in the West, they would not have much to spare. Earning a living was just that: working to survive.

And so God, their continual provider, gave them the Sabbath. While physical rest is important (and necessary), it was not the primary emphasis of the Sabbath. Instead, the point of taking a full day off every week was to remind them that, even when we contribute through work, it is *God* who provides. The Sabbath is both a proof and a reminder of this.

The Sabbath today

Today, the Sabbath hasn't changed.

When the early church switched from Saturday to Sunday, it was circumstantial. The important part of the story was that they *continued* to set aside a day to refocus themselves on God. The day was not important. The practice was.

And so it is still for us today. We have the Sabbath to remember who's in charge. We have the Sabbath to help us reflect on our place in the creation. And we have the Sabbath to hear, as servants, from our creator.

HOW TO USE THIS DEVOTIONAL

This devotional is written for two reasons. The first is to inspire new thoughts. I hope, as you read this, God gives you new thoughts about himself and your role in his world.

And second, this devotional is meant to be a catalyst for change. I've included a short notes section after each, to write down brief reflections. Unlike a journal, which is longer and designed to help you process your thoughts, the lines in this book are to help you *remember* your thoughts. When God speaks, no matter how dynamic, our brains are still prone to forget. And so writing insights down helps.

One your Sabbath each week, use this as a guide to reflect on your creator and the role he's set aside for you.

MEDITATIONS

READJUSTING JESUS

America is a great country.

Really, I'm an American. And I love it. But it's not the kind of place for sacrifice. America is more of a have-your-cake-and-eat-it-too kind of place. And that creates a special kind of abundance. An abundance the rest of the world values. And wants.

But I think, if we're not careful, we can let that view define how we understand Jesus' call.

At one point he tells his followers, "whoever does not take his cross and follow me is not worthy of me" (Matthew 10:38). Here, "cross" means "everything else we value."

In America, that stands for some pretty valuable things:

Freedom to speak
Freedom to choose
Freedom to build
Freedom to vote
Freedom to not

Freedom to succeed

Freedom to be famous (or private)

Are these things bad? Definitely not. Well…not unless they're too important to give up.

CONSIDER

If you were to look inside yourself—with no excuses and nothing off limits—would you find something you're not willing to give up? Write down the areas you struggle with, or are tempted by.

_____

_____

_____

_____

_____

_____

_____

_____

_____

_____

_____

_____

_____

_____

CONTENDERS

Jude, excited and bubbling over at life following Jesus, decides to write to others he's mentored and known. Except, things have gone sideways. They—the ones he's writing to—are not experiencing the joy he is. They're experiencing something much different. And in the process, they're becoming slaves again to sin and Satan.

Jude gives them four simple steps to fix this:

1. Build up your faith.
2. Pray.
3. Keep yourselves focused on God's love.
4. Wait for Jesus.

What's the common thread here? Discipline. All four are actions that take both effort and intentionality.

What's interesting is that Jude doesn't spiritualized the problem. Instead, he gets practical. He says, life is hard so buckle down and do the work. There are plenty of things out of our control. But some of our problems are sitting right in our own laps.

That, to me, is good news.

CONSIDER

What's been captivating your thoughts recently? And is it helping you build up your faith? Or pull it down? If the latter, what can you do today to turn it into the former? How can the bad be used for good?

_____

_____

_____

_____

_____

_____

_____

_____

_____

_____

_____

_____

_____

_____

_____

_____

_____

_____

"HAVE NO HEDGE"

While training his disciples, Jesus tells them to "have no fear" (Matthew 10:26). The fear he's referring to is of persecution and loss. And, in some cases, death. In other words, heavy things.

But how does that work? How does one 'have no fear'? Fear isn't a switch to be flipped on and off. If, for instance, Jesus told you, "have no fear," how exactly would you go about that?

The answer, Jesus says, comes from our perspective.

"Do not fear those who can kill [just] the body," but instead, fear those who can kill the body and the soul (10:28).

In other words, don't hedge. Don't keep one foot grounded with God while the other's still concerned about the world.

Because our fear is directly related to our anchor.

CONSIDER

What is God calling you to do that pushes you beyond your comfort zone? Is fear of that thing holding you back? Should it be?

_____

_____

_____

_____

_____

_____

_____

_____

_____

_____

_____

_____

_____

_____

_____

_____

_____

_____

_____

_____

THE COULD/SHOULD LINE

Coulds are plentiful. These are the things that life sets us up for. Taking a new job, because we've got the resume. Making a new deal, because we were in the right place at the right time. And, no doubt, God uses these coulds.

Shoulds, on the other hand, are different. These are the things just for us. They are not about opportunity as much as they are about *purpose*. In other words, they are less about what we can do, and more about what God has *placed* us to do.

Coulds come from us using our brains and our sweat. Shoulds come from us spending time with God, listening and obeying.

A good life is finding both.

CONSIDER

Are your coulds and shoulds balanced? Are there activities you're doing that fall into the could, but not the should category? Is there something God is putting on your heart that you've been putting off? Not sure? Ask him.

_____

_____

_____

_____

_____

_____

_____

_____

_____

_____

_____

_____

_____

_____

_____

_____

_____

_____

_____

_____

CHRISTIAN ARBITRAGE

In finance, arbitrage is a form of trading that capitalizes on an imbalance somewhere in the market. In other words, it's selling high in one area, while simultaneously buying low in another.

The interesting thing about arbitrage is that the more it's used, the less it's available. Using it corrects the market and brings equilibrium. It's kind of like a good sale: word gets around.

As followers of Jesus, we live in a world of spiritual arbitrage. Our trade is to go out into the world and spread the message. The discrepancy is the need: so many have not yet found their way back to their Father.

But then, one day, it will be different. The market will be corrected.

Jesus said, "the Good News about the Kingdom will be preached throughout the whole world, so that all nations will hear it, and then, finally, the end will come" (Matthew 24:14).

CONSIDER

Consider this past week. Were you involved in spreading the message of Jesus? Think about this coming week. What can you do to that end?

_____

_____

_____

_____

_____

_____

_____

_____

_____

_____

_____

_____

_____

_____

_____

_____

_____

_____

_____

GOSPEL NEGOTIATIONS

John 8 is a series of dialogs between Jesus and the bad guys. It's a somewhat confusing chapter, if only because Jesus seems to be winding them up. It's as if he's trying to be inflammatory. The setting is Jesus teaching in the temple. While the dialogs of John 8 are between him and the religious leaders, they are being overheard by the rest— the regular people.

Two things come out of this.

First, it's the regular people who are his audience. Not the religious leaders. It's the regular people who are hearing how Jesus' message stacks up against the standard they know and trust. And it's the regular people who are considering Jesus' answers.

Second, Jesus knows who his real audience is, and so he doesn't get side-tracked with objections. The religious leaders he was talking to weren't looking for the truth. They were looking for a win. They'd already made up their minds. Many in the crowd, however, were listening.

The first rule of negotiation is to know what you want to leave with. Everything gets measured against this. Jesus came to offer truth to those who wanted it. And, in John 8, that's exactly what he did.

CONSIDER

Think about the ideal encounter with an unbeliever. What is the number one thing you want them to take away from your life? What would you need to do (or ignore) to make sure that happens?

_____

_____

_____

_____

_____

_____

_____

_____

_____

_____

_____

_____

_____

_____

_____

_____

FIRST ASSIGNMENT: RAISE THE DEAD

"These twelve Jesus sent out, instructing them... 'Heal the sick, raise the dead, clean lepers, cast out demons.'"
– Jesus (from Matthew 10:5-15)

Jesus picks his twelve and then sends them out on their first assignment to, amongst other things, raise the dead? Seems pretty steep. First time out and all. And, is such an instruction even remotely realistic?

No, as it turns out. It's not. But that's the point. It's not realistic to us. Salvation is not a problem we can handle ourselves. Following God isn't something we do alone. And neither is going out and doing his work.

But for him...these things are no problem. These things are what he does.

The question for us is not *what*, but *who*. That is: *whose* name are we going out and doing work for?

CONSIDER

When it comes to the gospel, what are you afraid of? Is it talking to strangers? Is it those from a different worldview laughing at yours? Or is it that you'll make a mistake? How can God help you overcome this fear?

CORPORATE MISSIONARIES

There's an idea, in some circles, that the holiest vocation is to be a pastor or missionary. And these are good, no doubt. But they're not *more* important, or holy, than other work. Like, being an accountant or school teacher or construction worker. These are not lesser jobs.

That's because the label is not what's important. It's what you do with the label (or job) that matters. Here's what I mean. Everyone needs the gospel. Everyone needs to know someone who knows Jesus and is willing to talk about him.

But most people won't go looking for it. And when they do come in contact with a pastor, most people aren't ready to be transparent. Instead, they feel guilty. And they want to put on a good face.

But this doesn't happen when those same people are talking to their peers, day in and day out. Over a lunch meeting to discuss a contract. Drinks after work. Or one covering a shift to help another. In these cases, the filter is gone. People are honest.

Paul understood this when he said, "I entered their world and tried to experience things from their point of view. I've become just about every sort of servant there is in my attempts to lead those I meet into a God-saved life" (from 1 Corinthians 9:19-23).

The bottom line is Jesus came to us because we weren't coming to him. And then, he told us: go do the same.

CONSIDER

Do you think of yourself as a missionary? What parts of your day would change if you did?

_____

_____

_____

_____

_____

_____

_____

_____

_____

_____

_____

_____

THIS IS GOING TO HURT

People don't want to be sold to. They don't want to be pressured into a *yes*, when they're really just a *maybe*...if that. This is why the best salespeople don't sell. They offer. They find the clear win for both sides. And they're upfront about the downsides.

And sometimes it's those downsides that move the deal forward. Transparency and honesty about the risk. And you know it's a good deal when you can be completely honest about the downsides and still have a better upside. Because the risk or time or cost is worth it.

Jesus said, "If anyone wishes to come after me, he must deny himself, and take up his cross and follow me" (Matthew 16:24).

That is, according to Jesus, his followers must (1) put his desires before theirs, (2) embrace death, and (3) submit to a totally different path.

That's either the worse sales pitch ever...or the best.

CONSIDER

Here's an experiment: ask a friend or coworker, who's not a Christian, *why* they're not. Let them know you're not trying to start a fight, you simply want to hear from their side. Then, consider how it would be for them to give that up to become a Christian.

_____

_____

_____

_____

_____

_____

_____

_____

_____

_____

_____

_____

_____

_____

_____

_____

_____

_____

_____

_____

_____

FOR FIGHTING DRAGONS

To the point of being painful, the pattern is almost always the same. You get out of church—where you're holy, where you had spiritual conversations about spiritual things—and then you get into your car.

Here is where it usually goes south. Kids yelling, drivers swerving, you running yellow lights (which are red lights). Like muscle memory, you're back to your old self.

Are you a hypocrite? Maybe. Some of us are.

But most us, I think, aren't. Most of us are just stuck. We want to be the person we are at church…yet we are constantly pulled back to be the one in the car: the version of ourselves we don't want to be. What's the solution here? How do we become the good version that we want to be?

The answer is in something called self-talk. This is the running narrative we tell ourselves. It's us choosing to focus on the good (being intentional) over the bad (our default).

In Philippians, Paul gives an example of this when he says to "rejoice in the Lord always." That's not just a song or hyperbole. It's an instruction. It's something we're actually supposed to do—even when we don't feel like it.

The key here is to keep doing it, in spite of our mess ups.

It's to keep reminding ourselves: "I'm saved by grace, and so I show grace to others" (Ephesians 4:7, 29). Or, "My life is Christ's, and so dying is only gain" (Philippians 1:21). Or, "Is this what I should be caring about?" (Matthew 16:26).

CONSIDER

Think about the past week or two. Was there a time when you acted in a way you were not proud of? What truth can you practice telling yourself now that corrects this?

_____

_____

_____

_____

_____

_____

_____

_____

_____

_____

EULOGIZING JOB
DESCRIPTIONS

Here's a thought someone shared with me once: Nobody talks about job descriptions at funerals. Nobody talks about how well he maximized the 401(k), or how many hours she did or didn't put in at the office.

Instead, those of us left always talk about what that person did for us—how they used their life to make ours better.

As Christians, this is the essence of the Great Commission. Jesus told us to make connections with others, to develop relationships built on trust, and then to pass on the best part of life—him.

That's what "making disciples" is.

From Jesus: "Go to the people of all nations and make them my disciples. Baptize them in the name of the Father, the Son, and the Holy Spirit, and teach them to do everything I have told you. I will be with you always, even until the end of the world" (Matthew 28:19-20).

CONSIDER

What do you want to be remembered for? What do you need to start doing today to make that happen? And what do you need to quit doing today?

_____

_____

_____

_____

_____

_____

_____

_____

_____

_____

_____

_____

_____

_____

_____

_____

_____

_____

_____

MOST OF US CAN CALL OFF THE SEARCH

"Go home to your friends and tell them"
– Jesus (Mark 5:19)

Jesus teaches the crowds. So many had gathered, so great was his fame, that they were becoming dangerous. Jesus tells his disciples to cross the lake, and says he'll catch up shortly. But during the night, a storm comes. The disciples, still in the boat, begin to get desperate. Until they see, strangely, Jesus walking to them…on top of the water. Jesus makes the storm go away.

On reaching the other side, they find a man with freakish strength, possessed by demons, and terrorizing the local town. Jesus fixes him, too. And then, the man– overcome with Jesus and his power–asks if he too can go with Jesus. And in one of the most interesting parts of this narrative, Jesus tells him: *no.*

He tells him to go back to those who know him best, because that's where the greatest impact of Jesus' work will happen. In his master-strategist sort of way, God had already placed the man–prior even to his conversion–exactly where he wanted him.

Often it's like that for us, too. We don't always need to *leave* to follow. We just need to follow.

God has a way of working out the rest.

CONSIDER

Think about the unique position God has placed you in. What would following where you are now look like?

_____

_____

_____

_____

_____

_____

_____

_____

_____

_____

_____

_____

_____

_____

_____

HELPLESSNESS OF MINISTRY

I retiled my bathroom recently. At one point I had to make a quick run to the store. My three-year-old, Hadley, said, "I want to come!"

"Because," she added matter-of-factly: "I will help you."

Help me, I laughed to myself. This will definitely not be helpful. But then I thought, isn't this just like us and God? There's much to be done in the world. Stuff we see all around us. Yet, how much do *we* really contribute to it? We can make noise, and move things around. We can even knock things down. But are we really helping?

And still, God has us busy working. In fact, he's *called* us to work (Matthew 28:18-20). It's easy to forget how much of our work and results are really God's work and results.

When we got to the store, I stood at the aisle thinking. Almost immediately, a little voice came: "Can we go now, Dad?"

"Mmm hmm, just a minute."

"Okay. I'm going to count the tiles."

"Okay, yeah, good idea."

CONSIDER

What part of work stresses you out? Is it because you've done something wrong (if so, then confessing and repenting is right)? Or is it because you're holding too tightly to it? What part can you put back in God's hands?

_____

_____

_____

_____

_____

_____

_____

_____

_____

_____

_____

_____

_____

_____

"*Let not your hearts be troubled*"

– JESUS

TIMBRE (YOURS AND MINE)

Timbre (sounds like tam-ber) is what makes middle C on a piano sound different from the same C played on a guitar or on a trumpet. Timbre comes from the individual construction of the instrument. This is why in a band you often have different instruments playing the same notes and chords.

Doing the same thing is not synonymous with being the same thing.

And so it is in the church. God gives us personalities, a kind of timbre, and this doesn't go away when we become followers of him. It gets stronger.

For us to deny ourselves—the way we think, the unique way we see the world—is to deny the timbre God built in us.

For You shaped me, inside and out.
You knitted me together in my mother's womb
– Psalm 139:13

CONSIDER

What part of you just doesn't seem to fit in with those
around you? Think about how God created you,
specifically, and uniquely. What benefit can your
uniqueness bring to the church?

_____

_____

_____

_____

_____

_____

_____

_____

_____

_____

_____

_____

_____

_____

_____

_____

_____

_____

INTIMATE-ME

In Ephesians 6, Paul lists what he calls the 'armor of God.' It's all a metaphor for how to avoid sin. He gives lots of strong verbs like "be strong," "put on," and "take up."

But in a totally different letter to different people, he says something that seems almost at odds with this. In 1 Corinthians 6, talking about sexual temptation, he says to run.

Why *run*? Why not fight, like in Ephesians 6? The answer is found in the nature of sex itself.

Sex is about intimacy. And as people we are designed to be intimate. It's a core part of our existence. And it's what defines our relationships with each other, and with God.

All other sins are external, Paul says. But sexual sins are against the core of who we are–against our own ability to relate as human.

Don't you know that your body is the temple of the Holy Spirit who comes from God and dwells inside of you? You do

not own yourself. You have been purchased at a great price, so
use your body to bring glory to God!
— Paul (1 Corinthians 6:19-20)

CONSIDER

Intimacy is about boundaries: finding the right time for both "yes" and "no." Is there a relationship in your life that should be more (or less) intimate? What would you need to do to make this happen?

_____

_____

_____

_____

_____

_____

_____

_____

_____

_____

_____

_____

_____

_____

_____

_____

_____

THE BALANCE OF
BEING A SINNER

"I desire mercy, not sacrifice."
– Jesus (Matthew 9:13)

Jesus told those who accused him of spending too much time with immoral people: *you've gone too far.*

And actually, the comment wasn't made to Jesus. It was made to his followers. Because Jesus was in the process of teaching his followers to do this, too. Jesus didn't distance himself from sin. But, at the same time, he didn't indulge in it.

How did he do this? He put his priority on glorifying his father.

"I have come down from heaven," he said, "not to do my own will but the will of him who sent me" (Luke 6:38).

And so it is with us, his followers.

Our priority isn't what we can do (or not do)–our sacrifice. Instead, it's to see how much we can become like the one who saved us.

CONSIDER

Who is someone recently you didn't show mercy to when you should have? It can be someone you live with or work with, or simply a car in traffic. If you were to live that experience again, how would you change it?

_____

_____

_____

_____

_____

_____

_____

_____

_____

_____

_____

_____

_____

_____

_____

_____

_____

_____

_____

LAUGHING AT THE DEVIL

For many, he's a silly, red pitchforked cartoon. A scarecrow that the weaker ones still run from. Some of us don't even believe he's real.

But the Bible gives us a different picture:

"For Satan himself masquerades as an angel of light."
– 2 Corinthians 11:14

"Be alert and of sober mind. Your enemy the devil prowls around like a roaring lion looking for someone to devour."
– 1 Peter 5:8

"I have forgiven in the sight of Christ for your sake, in order that Satan might not outwit us. For we are not unaware of his schemes."
– 2 Corinthians 2:10-11

"In addition to all this, take up the shield of faith, with which you can extinguish all the flaming arrows of the evil one."
– Ephesians 6:16

The lesson here is that Satan is both real and relevant. He's a serious enemy. The good news: God is bigger, and better.

But our protection comes from God. Not from ourselves.

And there's a certain level of respect that should go with that.

CONSIDER

In what ways do you minimize Satan's existence? How could you show a healthier respect? What would change in your prayer life if you did?

_____

_____

_____

_____

_____

_____

_____

_____

_____

_____

_____

_____

_____

IT'S OKAY TO MOVE ON

"Do not throw your pearls to pigs"
– Jesus (Matthew 7:6)

Not everything works out. Not everyone accepts.

Jesus, our model for how to live, tells us when that happens…it's okay to move on.

There is, after all, a lot more to do.

"The harvest is plentiful," he says, "but the laborers are few" (Luke 10:2).

CONSIDER

Ask God to reveal to you who you should be praying for and seeking—and who you should move on from. Be specific. Write down names if you can.

TWO KINDS OF FAITH

"You of little faith"
– Jesus (Matthew 8:26)

The time, out on the lake, when Jesus stopped the boat from sinking, he turns to his disciples: "you of little faith." What's interesting about this story is that these are professionals, in danger in their own profession, and yet they still turn to Jesus.

So why didn't Jesus praise them for their faith? Because there are two kinds of faith. And one is better than the other.

The first kind is knowledge. Intellectually, they knew the right answer. They'd seen Jesus do miracles. It was a logical conclusion to ask for more. The second kind is emotional. It's about assurance–about knowing–even when knowledge isn't present.

Jesus, in his statement, was referring to the second. When you look around, you'll see that most people who claim Jesus are claiming the first kind of faith.

It's easy to tabulate. And to justify. It's low risk. But it's not life-changing.

Instead, it's the second kind of faith that actually makes a difference. That's the kind the centurion had, which is why his reaction was so different.

"When Jesus heard this, he was amazed…he said, 'I tell you, I haven't seen faith like this in all Israel!'" (Luke 7:9).

CONSIDER

What part of your faith is ridiculous by worldly standards? Is there a part? If not, should there be? Ask God to show you where your faith can be strengthened.

_____

_____

_____

_____

_____

_____

_____

_____

_____

_____

HOW DOES A PERSON FIND FAITH?

Last week's thought was about two different kinds of faith. The first was real, but shallow. The second was deeper. And it was the second kind that Jesus praised.

The real question is, how do you get the second kind? Conveniently, there are three step:

First, pick a side. This is about commitment. It's the "intellectual faith" from yesterday's post. It's not bad, per se. It's just not complete by itself.

Second, take a risk. This is about intensity. There's no point in picking a side if you never leave the sidelines. You need to get to a point where you will lose something valuable if you are wrong. Sometimes life throws this at us without our consent. Other times we're given the chance to make the decision.

Third, repeat. This is about teaching our brain what to believe. The more we do something, the more commonplace it becomes (I explore this more in my book, *Life Hacking Spiritual Disciplines*).

The truth is, none of this is easy. The first is hard. The second is scary. And the third takes discipline.

But Jesus said, "Narrow [is] the road that leads to life, and only a few find it" (Matthew 7:14).

This is the only path that's worth it.

CONSIDER

What kind of risk can you take? And who is in your life to keep you accountable, and to keep watch for you for when you start slipping? If no one, what can you do to find someone?

_____

_____

_____

_____

_____

_____

_____

_____

_____

_____

_____

_____

_____

_____

HOW TO BE A
CONTRARIAN

How to be a contrarian? Answer: Give grace, accept grace, and believe it is the best thing for everyone you meet.

***

Meritocracy is the standard of our world: You get out what you put in.

When the first church "turned the world upside down" (Acts 17:6), it wasn't because they were causing trouble. It was because they were undoing the established meritocracy. They were spreading the gospel. They were telling everyone: there is someone who wants to pay for you.

***

"Gospel" and "grace" are in just about every sermon. They are common words. But their implication isn't.

When you show others grace, there is a backlash. It changes the expectation. Judgment is no longer passable. The hammer is no longer justified.

Most people don't like that. But then again, Jesus said, most people won't choose this way.

CONSIDER

In what ways can you rebel against meritocracy? What would you have to do to show grace in a way that causes people to talk about you behind your back? Write that down. Then go do it.

_____

_____

_____

_____

_____

_____

_____

_____

_____

_____

_____

_____

THESE ARE NOT THE FINEST THINGS

When I was young(er), I remember thinking about how nice it would be to share coffee, early in the morning, with my wife, whoever she'd be. When I thought of the good life, I thought of little things like that. Basically, I thought of a Pottery Barn commercial.

Today, in real life, my wife doesn't even like the smell of coffee. And, for her, mornings are a result of the fall. So when I get up, early in the morning, before the kids, and drink my coffee or tea, it's just me. Alone.

But that's okay. Because what I learned is that Pottery Barn commercials are completely ridiculous. There are things that make for a good life, but it's never stuff like that.

Here's how I learned to tell the difference: I compare my life *with* it to my life *without* it. When I feel the same in both cases, I know it's not something that matters.

When something has to go, it's really good to know which to pick.

CONSIDER

In your mind's eye, look around at the parts that make up your day. Write down a few of the big ones. What would your life look like without them? Which ones are dead weight? And what can you put in their place?

DID YOU HEAR THE ONE...

Did you ever hear the one about the Promised Land? God said to Abraham, *here it is. It's all yours*. And then what?

Nothing.

Abraham lived to be old. His son Isaac lived to be old. And his grandson, Jacob. Then his great-grandson, Joseph–he lived to be old, too. Four-hundred years pass by. Still not much to show.

Then Moses comes along. He gathers all the people (a lot by now). They escape Egypt only to wander around for a few decades eating bread on the ground. And not in the promised land. Then, finally, Abraham's children begin settling in. After half a millennium.

What happened? And why did God make it seem like it was a done deal when he originally told Abraham?

Because, in many ways...*it was*. This was the case then, and it's the case now. The in-between stuff is never a challenge to God. Instead, it's a *chance* for us.

Paul, talking about Abraham, said, "That is why it depends on faith." Abraham was "fully convinced that God was able to do what he had promised" (Romans 4:16, 21). And in the process, he grew to be more like God.

That's what God's giving us.

CONSIDER

What is standing in between the promises from Scripture, and your life today? Write down challenges that can be turned into chances.

MINUTIAE, ETC.

In Basketball, you win by getting the ball in your hoop more times than the other guys. Pretty simple. There are other rules, too, like how many steps you can take, or how you can touch other players. But those other rules are all in service of the greater: getting more baskets.

But here's the interesting part: When the game's over, almost nobody talks about the big thing–how many points were scored. The discussion always finds the little things. Fouls, players' attitudes.

And many times, these are the things that are remembered.

Paul writes it like this: "Run in such a way as to get the prize" (1 Corinthians 9:24).

It's not just about the prize. It's about how we get there, too.

CONSIDER

What impression do you leave on others? Is it one you'd be comfortable getting leaked to your boss, or family, or church? What part of your race can you change so that you can be proud of that impression?

_____

_____

_____

_____

_____

_____

_____

_____

_____

_____

_____

_____

_____

_____

_____

_____

_____

_____

_____

_____

_____

_____

_____

"LET IT BE"

"Let it be done for you as you have believed"
– Jesus (Matthew 8:13)

Is your pattern of obedience based on fear (it'll be bad if I don't) or expectation (this will be good)? It's easy to confuse the two when following people, because their physical presence has a way of motivating.

Personally, I don't want the shame of disappointing a good leader, often, just as much as I don't want to miss the promise they're giving me.

But when it comes to following God–who I cannot see or touch–this difference becomes apparent.

The centurion was able to leave Jesus and still trust him because his faith was not tied to fear, but to expectation.

He believed Jesus could and would do it.

The lesson for us: If you're following based on fear, your faith will always be small.

But if you're following based on expectation, it will outgrow you, many times over.

CONSIDER

Are you ready for your faith to be judged? Or are there still more improvements you want to make? What would an impressive faith look like to you? How can you begin becoming that person today?

_____

_____

_____

_____

_____

_____

_____

_____

_____

_____

_____

_____

_____

_____

_____

_____

_____

_____

SERVING SERVICE

Jesus replied, "They do not need to go away. You give them something to eat."

"We have here only five loaves of bread and two fish," they answered.

"Bring them here to me," he said (Matthew 14:16-18).

We don't all have the gift of service. But, yet, we're all called to serve. It's always hard to serve people we don't like. But the more we're conditioned to do it, the easier it becomes—even for those we don't like.

When you become a person people want to serve, you help them by teaching them what service feels like. In other words, by being easy to serve, you become the catalyst to help others learn to serve.

Which, by the way, it what Jesus did.

CONSIDER

What is your spiritual gift? Have you ever thought about your gift as being a catalyst for others to use theirs? How can you use your spatial gift more?

"Be sure of this, I am with you always"

- JESUS

A NEW AGE WITH AN OLD PROBLEM

"See if there be any grievous way in me, and lead me in the way everlasting!"
– Psalm 139:24

New Age Spiritualism sounds like it would be off-beat. Something for weird people. But it's actually quite common.

In New Age Spirituality you are bad on the inside until you discover that you are really good. Then, through the right mindset, you blossom into a better you.

Contrast this with Christianity. In Christianity, God values you, but you alone are not good. It is restoration between you and God that makes you good.

In the one, your self-doubt and bad behavior is imagined or out-grown. In the other, you are lifted out by the only one who has a track record of success.

One option takes ego. The other takes, necessarily, *less* ego.

CONSIDER

One way to check for pride is to look at which parts of your testimony would be discredited if you were. In other words, which parts of your gospel story are about you, and which parts are about God? What would your story look like if it were completely about God?

_____

_____

_____

_____

_____

_____

_____

_____

_____

_____

_____

_____

_____

_____

_____

_____

_____

_____

TEACHING A TEACHER

"Where are your interests?"

In statement form, Jesus posed this question to those questioning him (John 7). For his unusual and somewhat taboo methods, the people around him—the *authorities* around him—were challenging his credibility.

If ever there was someone qualified to defend his actions, it seems it would be Jesus. But he didn't do that. Instead, he walked them through the right way to think.

Who am I pointing to? he asked. If it's me, then you've got the right to criticize. But if I'm pointing to the Father in heaven, then what's your argument?

It's the same for us.

We're all messy and sinful. Not much argument there. But how do we know when one of us is on the right track or not? How do we know when that mess and sin is throwing off the work of the kingdom?

The answer is, as Jesus pointed out: What are they interested in? Is it God, or is it something else?

CONSIDER

Who does your life point to? Do you leverage God to look good? Or do you leverage yourself so that others look to God? If you need to change something, what would it be?

_____

_____

_____

_____

_____

_____

_____

_____

_____

_____

_____

_____

_____

_____

_____

_____

_____

_____

GOOD WORK IS A MISFIT

Good work is hard.

Introducing people to Jesus is hard.

Maintaining difficult relationships is hard.

Living consistently is hard.

Living as a transparent follower of Jesus is hard.

Doing something that makes a big difference in someone else's life is hard.

But…if these things weren't hard, they'd be done already.

So, in some way, it's *good* they're hard. Because that means we get to help.

Jesus said, "a large crop is in the fields, but there are only a few workers" (Matthew 9:37).

The hard work is worth it.

CONSIDER

What is your hard work? Do you know? If you do, write it down. Each and every day, write it down again so that you never forget to keep doing it. And if you don't know, take some time to ask God to show it to you.

_____

_____

_____

_____

_____

_____

_____

_____

_____

_____

_____

_____

_____

_____

_____

_____

_____

_____

_____

_____

_____

_____

_____

_____

_____

_____

FAKE ROLEX

Have you ever come across a really good fake Rolex? In a real Rolex, the second hand 'sweeps' by at eight ticks a second. This is because the inside (the "movement") is full of gears and cranks. There's no battery. But in a good fake, that 'sweep' may only be about five ticks per second.

Can you tell the difference between five and eight ticks per second? Probably not.

Most of us can't unless we really know what to look for. Plus, when we compare buying a real Rolex ($8,000) to a good fake ($500), the good fake becomes pretty tempting.

But when you go to cash in, a certified Rolex dealer isn't going to take the fake, no matter how many other people it fools.

***

Jesus said, "Not everyone who says to me, 'Lord, Lord,' will enter the kingdom of heaven" (Matthew 7:21).

This doesn't mean we can't have certainty in our standing with God.

It just means we can't fake it.

CONSIDER

How can those who know you most tell if you are a true and legitimate child of God? And the opposite, what evidence does their life show? And how can you encourage and support them in this way?

_____

_____

_____

_____

_____

_____

_____

_____

_____

_____

_____

_____

_____

_____

_____

_____

WHY ARE YOU A CHRISTIAN?

If were you to ask a Hindu or a Muslim or a person of another religion why they were that religion, most would say something along the lines of: *it's what I was given*. They may feel passionate about it, even be able to defend it. But, for most of them, it's something they inherited from their parents.

What's different about Christianity is that it isn't like this at all. As a matter of fact, it's not Christianity if it was inherited. That's because at its core Christianity is a *choice*. And that is one of the things that makes it so special.

CONSIDER

If someone asked you why you are a Christian, what would you say? Could you explain it in the way a normal person would understand in about 10 seconds? If not, do you think others really understand why you're a Christian? Take a few moments to write it out.

DON'T BURN BRIDGES, NAPALM THEM

Sometimes we have to burn bridges. Like with toxic relationships. The problem is that a burned bridge can be rebuilt. And that's not always good. The better option?

Napalm them.

Hear me out. Continuing the metaphor: when you napalm a bridge, it's absolute. It's overkill. There is just no going back. And as a result, napalming bridges is a lot more serious.

If you commit to only napalming bridges—making the disconnection so obvious and clear that it could never be reconnected—then you'll be careful about who you do this for.

Some relations are truly bad and you need to be separated. Go ahead and napalm those.

But a lot of shaky relationships just need some healthy space. Don't burn those. Just back away for a while.

CONSIDER

Are there toxic relationships in your life that are dragging you down? How could you safely and responsibly separate yourself from these bad relationships?

_____

_____

_____

_____

_____

_____

_____

_____

_____

_____

_____

_____

_____

_____

_____

_____

_____

_____

_____

_____

OFTEN GOD ISN'T CALLING US TO DO BIG THINGS

Moses spent most of his life dealing with little things.

He was born into royalty. He grew up with a passionate but idealistic view of people. That got him into trouble when he thought he was helping his brothers by killing an Egyptian. They saw him as a hypocrite.

Then he ran. He spent the next four decades herding sheep. It was only then that God called him to do something. Eighty years in.

Jesus–the savior of humanity–lived the first thirty of his thirty-three years doing normal stuff.

Most of the Old Testament prophets got a message from God once, or a few times at most. It wasn't an occupation for them, it was an exception.

Here's the point: for most of our lives, God isn't calling us to do big things. He's calling us to do little things well. It's all of the little stuff (the boring stuff) where we develop who we are for those big moments (the parts people write about).

It's the ordinary that defines extraordinary. And with that, it's in our interest to do the best ordinary work we can.

CONSIDER

Do you find yourself cutting corners on the little things? Do you believe that's affecting your character? If not, why? And if you are, how can you do a better job at doing the little things right?

THE PARADOX OF MAKING PEACE

"Blessed are the peacemakers"
– Jesus (Matthew 5:9)

For most of us, peace equals calm. It's when we're at rest.
But that's the outcome, the result. The getting there is a
different thing entirely.

The picture of peace that Jesus gave us was not
magical, but balanced. "Forgive, if you have anything
against anyone" (Mark 11:25) and "Whatever you wish
that others would do to you, do also to them" (Matthew
7:12).

It takes effort–sometimes a lot–to make peace.
Sometimes, even, it's the hardest thing we will do.

Other times still, it will cost us more than we're
comfortable losing.

Jesus said: "In me you may have peace. In the world
you will have tribulation. But take heart; *I have overcome
the world*" (John 16:33).

It does no good to run away from this fight. No matter how hard it is.

No other alternative is better.

CONSIDER

Is there a difficult peace in your life you're avoiding? What can you do to address it? How can you pray about it? What is the benefit that will come from it?

_____

_____

_____

_____

_____

_____

_____

_____

_____

_____

_____

_____

_____

_____

_____

_____

_____

iDOL

My friend Andrew recently preached a message from Acts. In the passage, Paul confronts the idol worshipers in Athens.

If you've been in church for any length of time, it's clear where this is going: *What are the idols in your life?* We get it. Anything that gets between you and God is an idol. My car, my money, my job.

But then, in front of us all, he confessed. His own idol: his phone. And, holy crap, it hit me.

That's me.

When I call, you come. No matter what you're doing. I don't care if you're in the middle of a conversation with another person, or voicing a prayer to God—my ding requires your response.

That's not the problem of faraway men in a faraway land. That's me. Is there any better idol today than the one we charge every morning and carry around in our pocket all day?

When we think about revival in our country, we think about everybody coming back to church.

And maybe it is.

Or…maybe revival just looks a bit more like a flip-phone.

CONSIDER

What are the things in your life that would be difficult to live without? And what are the things in your life that seem to always have your attention? Does God have that same pull on you? And do your actions reflect that?

_____

_____

_____

_____

_____

_____

_____

_____

_____

_____

_____

_____

_____

_____

_____

IN THE LAND OF CRIMINALS

"Go out and train everyone you meet, far and near, in this way of life"
– Jesus (Matthew 28:19)

It's easy—and natural, even—to complain and be down about the bad.

I live in New Orleans. We often rank on things like "most murders per capita."

But stopping here leaves a lot on the table.

That's because love and forgiveness make a much bigger impact in the places the need is most obvious.

So the real question is: where is the most obvious need, and are you there?

CONSIDER

What big bad things in your life need the gospel? How can you become that messenger?

A NOTE ON DIVINE INTERRUPTIONS

"Go and announce to them that the kingdom of heaven is near."
– Jesus (Matthew 10:7)

My friend Rich spent a good chunk of his career as a manager. He learned something one day—something he told me—which changed the way I looked at work.

Divine interruptions.

I'm a productivity person. I like to get things done. And I plan out my day. But it never goes according to plan. People happen.

So I've got two options: Fight it, avoid it, ignore it. Or…treat it like God intended it to happen.

When we do the first, we get more of our own stuff done. Which is not a bad thing. But when we do the second, we get more of *God's* stuff done. And this, of course, is the better thing.

Divine interruptions are a way to get involved in Kingdom work wherever we are, whatever we're doing.

So, how do you spot them?

Here's the trick: *you don't*. You just treat every opportunity as if it were a chance to encourage, teach, learn, serve, or give. And then it becomes it.

CONSIDER

Think about the interruptions you've had over the last few days? Did you treat them like they were sent from God? How do you need to prepare for this coming week to start thinking about them like that?

_____

_____

_____

_____

_____

_____

_____

_____

_____

_____

_____

_____

_____

_____

FRACTAL LIVING

"He has committed to us the message of reconciliation"
– Paul (2 Corinthians 5:19)

A fractal is a shape who's parts are the same as the whole. A six-sided snowflake that's made up of six-sided arms. A Douglas Fir Christmas tree with cone-shaped branches. And the Moon orbiting the Earth while the Earth orbits the Sun.

The benefit of a fractal is that the system works at all levels.

The differences then, are not in value, but in application. A railroad spike may be shaped just like the nails behind my picture frames (functionally they're doing the same thing: bonding two disjointed pieces together). But their applications are quite different. And it's the difference that matters.

This is the Christian life.

The impact we make is not a reflection of our placement (or scale). Instead, our impact hangs on us doing what we were put here to do. Whether you work at a church, are a staffer at the White House, or hold a sign under the bridge, God's given us each a job with the potential to alter eternity.

That job, fortunately, is pretty simple.

As Paul writes, it's to keep telling the story.

CONSIDER

How can you tell your gospel story in your context? Even if you work in a place that forbids it, you can still tell your story. Ask God to show you one person this week you can share with.

_____

_____

_____

_____

_____

_____

_____

_____

_____

_____

_____

_____

_____

"HI, LITTLE BOY"

"Hi, little boy."

Graham cut his eyes at me as a four-year-old stranger stood waving at him. When the boy left, Graham (who was both unamused and also *five* years old) told me, "he thinks I'm little. I'm not."

My son was offended because in his mind "little boy" was a put-down.

But this smiling little four-year-old stranger saw things differently. In a world of adults, he saw someone else, just like him, and he was happy about it.

The funny thing is, we don't outgrow this. Even into adulthood, we continue to believe that everyone we meet sees the world as we do. As if they're making all the same assumptions. But this is almost never the case. And the result usually looks something like conflict: insults, fights, and so on.

But what if our first assumption wasn't that they're seeing what we're seeing. What if our first assumption–the one we give the benefit of the doubt to–was that they aren't trying to hurt us? How many of our daily headaches would evaporate with that one change? (And how many new friends would we make?)

My guess is, at least a few. And that, I think, is worth it.

CONSIDER

The next time someone offends you—be it big or small— how could you change your default reaction (offense) and assume they don't mean you harm? And what would be the benefit of doing this?

_____

_____

_____

_____

_____

_____

_____

_____

_____

_____

_____

_____

_____

_____

_____

_____

*"Wisdom is justified
by her deeds"*

- JESUS

THE ECONOMICS OF GIVING VS TAKING

Taking is like a social debt. What I do affects how my neighbors live. And the more globalized our world becomes, the more my neighbors become people in Africa and Asia and other places.

Giving, on the other hand, is more like an investment. It's not always one-to-one. Not everyone you help will help you back. So it's hard to measure in the short term.

But have you ever noticed how things get better over time? With the exception of bitterness, we remember the good things. So much so that we've even come up with a name for it: nostalgia.

The reason we act this way is because this is how God designed us. Sin comes from (our) taking. Salvation from (God's) giving. It's good to give.

Warren Buffet, the famous investor, reportedly makes every investment as if he plans to never sell it. Whether it's literally true or not, that kind of philosophy has worked pretty well for him. $80 billion well.

The point: taking is finite. We can only handle so much. But giving is infinite. The more we do it, the better those around us are. The more we begin to think like our Creator. And, ironically, the stronger we become. Living like this is a long-game. The key here is to focus on the process and not the outcome. The giving, not the getting.

***

One more thought: Taking is not the same as accepting. Taking leaves a void, while accepting validates someone else's giving.

CONSIDER

If you created a social balance sheet: do you take (not accept) more? Or give more? What are ways can you begin giving more?

_____

_____

_____

_____

_____

_____

_____

MOST OF US ARE WRONG

It's okay to disagree.

Mainly because there's very little we know for sure. Stuff like: God is good. That's one we know.

But most of the time, we don't disagree with each other on foundational things like this. Instead, we tend to disagree on process issues. In other words, we disagree on the how, not the what. As Christians, we all agree we should be a witness to the world–but what path do we take here? That's where it gets jumbled.

What's not okay is to re-value a person based on their opinions or approach. Even if they're wrong.

The trouble is that's our default. If they don't do things like us, they're not "one of us."

But, of course they're not. They're one of God's.

That's all any of us are.

CONSIDER

Think about some things you disagree strongly with other believers on. Are they mission-critical? Is there biblical support for the disagreement? And is your disagreement hurting or helping the kingdom?

_____

_____

_____

_____

_____

_____

_____

_____

_____

_____

_____

_____

_____

_____

_____

_____

_____

_____

_____

EMPATHY OF A LOG

"Why do you see the speck that is in your brother's eye, but do not notice the log that is in your own eye?"
– Jesus (Matthew 7:3)

Jesus tells us to address our own mess first. Hypocrisy is a big deal.

But I don't believe hypocrisy is the root of his issue here. I think the deeper reason Jesus told us to look at ourselves first, is because that's how we develop empathy for others.

Empathy is when you can feel what others feel. When you address your own issues first, you not only understand the truth of the matter, you work through the emotional baggage that comes with it.

Most of us, in some form or another, have a concept of right and wrong. And if not, there's google. What we don't need are more facts.

Instead, what we need are people who've made it through who can tell us where not to step. That's what empathy is. And that's who we become when we look at ourselves first.

CONSIDER

When you consider the sins of others, do you find yourself hoping they overcome them? Leaning in to their success? Or do you tend to fixate on the negative, disciplinarian aspects? How could you become more empathetic to those you know struggling in sin?

_____

_____

_____

_____

_____

_____

_____

_____

_____

_____

_____

_____

_____

_____

_____

_____

THE LIMITS OF LIFE

Recently Dr. Elisabetta Barbi of the University of Rome did a study on the length of life. Her findings? "If there's a fixed biological limit, we are not close to it."

My wife's grandfather is 95. Every time I see him, I ask him questions. (My goal is to make it to triple-digits.) He's happy and cheerful. But his advice on the matter is "don't."

On the other hand, there are some people who live only a few years. Nate Saint (33) and Jim Elliot (29) both died bringing the gospel to places that had never heard it. And more recently, Nabeel Qureshi had an incredible trajectory before him, except he died from cancer, at 34. I'm 34.

There is much we cannot control. And it's easy to become cynical about that.

But there are a few things we can control. Like, what we do with today. Michael Crichton wrote that all of life "has the same shape of a single day."

Life isn't limited by length, it's limited by depth. And fortunately, that is something we can control.

CONSIDER

A sobering thought, but if this were your last week, what would you do differently? Write one or two things down. And if this *isn't* your last week, can you still do those things?

_____

_____

_____

_____

_____

_____

_____

_____

_____

_____

_____

_____

_____

_____

The article, "The plateau of human mortality: Demography of longevity pioneers," by Elisabetta Barbi appeared in *Science* on June 29, 2018 in volume 360, issue 6396, page 1459-1461.

THE TIMES WHEN HERESY ISN'T SO BAD

In the world of theology, heresy is the equivalent of failure. It is often demonized—heretics get kicked out of the church. And in many cases, this is a good thing.

But I think if we leave it there, we're missing something important.

Ever tried to explain the Trinity? If you've used an analogy, you almost certainly committed a heresy. Just the way it goes.

But were you trying to change church doctrine in the process? I seriously doubt it. You were probably trying to understand it and teach it.

The thing is, with growth comes an inherent risk. And if we're too afraid of that risk, then we never grow—which is the exact opposite of what Jesus wants for us.

It's okay to be a heretic from time to time if your goal is to learn and grow. What matters with heresy is whether you recognize it as heresy, or as a new truth.

CONSIDER

What areas can you stretch into? Here's a hint: start with an area you are passionate about. How can you push that area further? Write down the risks associated. Next, write down the worst case scenarios for each risk. Then, ask yourself if it's worth it.

_____

_____

_____

_____

_____

_____

_____

_____

_____

_____

_____

_____

_____

_____

_____

_____

_____

_____

_____

JUST ABOUT EVERYONE DISAGREES WITH ME ON THIS

I don't believe there is ever a time God wants us to wait.

Not patience, but waiting.

Patience is a different issue. That's about discipline. Waiting—or inaction—is about motivation.

Let me explain. Whenever we do something new, there are usually a ton of steps. God's put something on your heart, and the vision you see is somewhat mature. It's a complete thing.

But today, before it's a thing you can talk about, you're just at step-one…if that much. One of the biggest objections we face to following God is "not ready yet." But God doesn't call us to be ready, he calls us to be willing and to follow.

The ready happens on the way.

CONSIDER

Is there something God's put on your heart you're not prepared for yet? Big or small, write that down. Then, ask God if now is the time to do it.

_____

_____

_____

_____

_____

_____

_____

_____

_____

_____

_____

_____

_____

_____

_____

_____

_____

_____

_____

_____

_____

THE ANTI-ANXIOUS PATH

"Do not be anxious"
— Jesus (Matthew 6:25)

The simplicity of this statement does not imply the simplicity of the solution. Anxiety is not a measure of spiritual maturity, or lack thereof. It's a weapon from the evil one. And it's best to think about it like this.

Anxiety at its core is a void. And so our job is to find the right tools to help us replace that void. For some, the best tool for anxiety is simply a better mindset. For others, it may be the right prescription bottle. That's okay.

Knowing the difficulty we'd have here, Jesus gives us a guideline to focus on. A few verses later, he concludes with: in all things, "put the kingdom first."

Not everything gets fixed in this life. (Jesus did not promise we won't have anxiety here.) But Isaiah 65 and Revelation 21 both show us a world completely restored. When anxiety will be truly gone.

We know this is coming.

But today, our path is to practice, to learn, to forgive (others and ourselves), and to not give up. That's how we focus on the kingdom. And that's how we work toward Jesus' instruction.

The command is not simplistic. But it is a reflection of hope. Of the bigger (and better) thing to come.

CONSIDER

It's best to prepare for anxiety *before* you get anxious. Write down topics or specific issues that typically cause you anxiety. Next, write down truths from Scripture that correspond to these anxieties. And finally, memorize these truths.

_____

_____

_____

_____

_____

_____

_____

_____

_____

_____

_____

_____

A CASE STUDY IN GETTING BLESSINGS

"Wherever you are, be all there."
– Jim Elliot

Classic stories: David against the lion–he shouldn't have won. Against the giant: same thing. And against all the others more qualified than he to be king. Again.

So what did David do that set him apart?

He was simply ready long before blessings were even on the table. He was committed to keeping his sheep safe. So when the lion came, he already knew what to do. On the heels of that, he saw the giant, not fearfully as the soldier did, but as just another enemy with a fatal weakness. And finally, to be chosen as king, he spent years letting his character be changed in the small areas–a decision that God ultimately credited.

Some thousand years later, Paul would write: "Whatever you do, do it…for the Lord" (Colossians 3:23).

That's the point of blessings.

They don't enable the work–they follow it.

CONSIDER

Blessings are good. But focusing too much on them can distract us from the work. Do you find yourself focusing often on blessings or results? What would change in your work if you focused only on doing good work, regardless of the results?

_____

_____

_____

_____

_____

_____

_____

_____

_____

_____

_____

_____

_____

_____

_____

_____

THE WORLD IS
IMPRESSED

It matters what the world thinks about us, because we're supposed to be their salt and light. In 1 Timothy 3:7, Paul says that one of the qualifications for a church leader is that "he have a good reputation with outsiders."

What this doesn't mean is that we bend to their standards.

But what it *does* mean is that if we follow God and his holiness, God's standards will make a positive impression on the world.

We saw a giant case study for this a few centuries back. And it went over amazingly well. The founders of the United States were a collection of men influenced by the Gospel. Many of them were not true followers (Ben Franklin and Thomas Jefferson, to name two). But, yet, our laws—and even our currency—saw its influence.

Here's the point: the way we reach the world is by first getting our stuff right on the inside. When we do that, it has a way of bleeding out and influencing those around us.

The gospel isn't about coercion.

It's about influence.

CONSIDER

What kind of influence are you leaving? Does it point others to God? If not, how can you change your influence to do so?

_____

_____

_____

_____

_____

_____

_____

_____

_____

_____

_____

_____

_____

_____

_____

_____

_____

HOW DO YOU ANSWER A FOOL ACCORDING TO HIS FOLLY?

"Answer not a fool according to his folly, lest you be like him yourself."
- Proverbs 26:4

How do you answer a fool according to his folly? In the way that will push him closest to Jesus.

That may mean a firm hand. Other times it may mean silence. Other times still, it may take patience, teaching, and forgiveness.

There's not a cookie-cutter, apply-just-this-way answer. Well, unless we say: *Listen to the Spirit's prompting and follow accordingly.*

So what does that mean?

It means we're ambassadors for the King. The fool is in rebellion. But the King still longs for him. And so we answer with the fool in mind, not his folly.

CONSIDER

When Jesus died on the cross, it was for, as Paul says, those who were still his enemies. He loved his enemies as if they were sons and daughters. Do you feel this way about those who hate you? What would it take—on your end—for you to begin moving in that direction?

JUST LIKE GLASS

"Be as shrewd as snakes and harmless as doves."
-Jesus (Matthew 10:16b)

About 150 years ago, a man in Paris was experimenting with a new kind of glass and produced the first version of tempered glass.

The key to creating tempered glass is to heat it to over 1,000 degrees Fahrenheit and then, during that time when it's super-hot, mold it in its final shape. What's interesting is the state of the final product. Normal glass has virtually no internal stress. It's at ease.

But tempered glass is different. Not only has it been through a grueling process, but once it's cooled, it's under a perpetual tension. And it is this tension that causes it to be mostly harmless when it breaks (unlike regular glass which breaks into dangerous shards).

Tempered glass is a lot like our own spiritual growth.

Sometimes God allows rough things to happen to us, because he's in the process of creating something that's going to be stronger. And when things break—sometimes we break—we don't shatter into a mess and hurt those we love.

CONSIDER

Take a moment to thank God for all the tempering and strengthening he's done in your life—even when it's been difficult. Write down a few memories that come to mind.

_____

_____

_____

_____

_____

_____

_____

_____

_____

_____

_____

_____

_____

_____

_____

_____

_____

_____

EVOLUTION IS A
METAPHOR

Smart people explain things in systems.

Evolution is a metaphor for order. It's a needed metaphor, because—as the world tells us—God doesn't exist. At least not in the: I created everything and have a plan for you sense. So Evolution, while described as a process of nature, really functions as a God-replacement.

But…why the extra work? Why create a new concept to explain away God? Because God requires something extra from us that Evolution doesn't.

God requires moral accountability.

In economics, the law of supply and demand symbolically tells us that there are consequences for what we do. But with God, we don't determine those consequences. The very nature of man's problem is that he relies on his own standard.

And so, the cycle continues. We need something that will give us what God gives us, but without the implications of God. We need our cake, and we need to eat it, too.

CONSIDER

Are there parts of your own narrative that don't require
you to depend on God? How would these areas be
different if they were dependent on God?

_____

_____

_____

_____

_____

_____

_____

_____

_____

_____

_____

_____

_____

_____

_____

_____

_____

_____

THE THING ABOUT GRACE THAT EVERYONE FORGETS

Grace is the theme of the gospel message. It's the logic behind God coming to redeem us. And it's how we can experience the good in spite of our bad.

But there's something everyone seems to forget. If today I'm good at my job, or my marriage–earning my keep, as it were—what happens tomorrow when I'm having an off week (or year)? Is everything tallied together like a giant ledger?

No.

We remember what we see, and we forget the past.

But grace undoes that.

Grace pushes us to forgive and accept even if its not merited. And, as it is sometimes the case, when we've forgotten what we've forgotten.

CONSIDER

Pause for a moment to internalize the implications of grace. What areas of your life can you give others grace? What areas of your life can you give yourself grace?

_____

_____

_____

_____

_____

_____

_____

_____

_____

_____

_____

_____

_____

_____

_____

_____

_____

_____

WHAT'S NEXT

Regardless of where you are in your spiritual growth, what's important is to keep moving *forward*. Moving forward is simply that: you continuing to grow closer to God.

There are two ways you can think of this. The first movement is more days. And the second is more time.

More days

'More days' can be moving from once a week to two or three times. Or from two or three times to every day. Or even from once a day to several times per day.

Devotionals are helpful. But ultimately, this kind of movement requires you to branch out. Devotionals are guides to help you think about God.

To move forward, begin cultivating a practice of going directly to God. If you were shipwrecked on a deserted island, would you have all the tools you need to spend time with God? By working to pare down what you are dependent on, you free yourself to expand in frequency.

More time

The second 'more' is in time. This is when you're going from a short time to a longer time.

There are several ways you can do this. You can read longer passages, or more passages. You can split your time into segments: Begin with praise and thanksgiving, move into reading, then spend some time meditating on God's voice, followed by more reading and prayer requests.

The biggest challenge to adding more time, however, is not what to do, but what *not* to do. If you don't schedule the time by actually putting it on your calendar, scaling up your time can be difficult.

Prayer Guide

I've created a guide. A lot of people I talk to struggle with where to start—and then how to stay focused. My goal in this little guide is to fix both of these. You can find it on my website, joefontenot.info/resources.

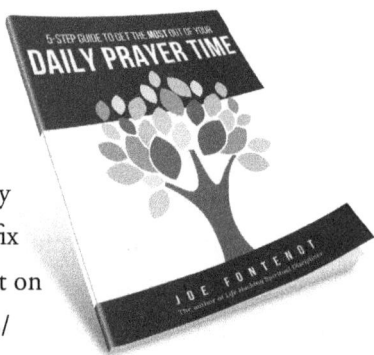

One last thing

The temptation for so many of us is to look to others to gauge our own progress. But, we know this doesn't work. This is like comparing the fuel economy of a pickup truck to a Prius. On that scale, the truck will always fail. But it was designed for a different progress. Keep your progress on your own scale. Are you moving forward according to *you*. That's the key.

In all of this, one of the strongest tools you'll have is consistency. This was a cornerstone outcome of the research from my first book, *Life Hacking Spiritual Disciplines*, for building a routine.

Regardless of set backs, keep pushing forward.

ABOUT THE AUTHOR

Joe is the author of two other books, *Life Hacking Spiritual Disciplines*, a look at the habits it takes to build spiritual discipline, and *Minimalist Marketing*, the guide for churches and nonprofits to reach their audience without a marketing budget.

Joe is the marketing strategist for New Orleans Baptist Theological Seminary. And prior to this, he spent a decade in international logistics, helping NGO's move their cargo all over the world.

He lives in New Orleans with his wife, Kristin, and their two little ones.

FIVE ROUND ROCKS

Five Round Rocks is a resource for the church. Learn more at fiveroundrocksmedia.com.

THANKS TO...

Kristin, because you always tell me when I'm saying something dumb. Stacey, for fixing all my words. Sam, for making my art better. And Jack and Joe, for always being encouraging.

WANT MORE?

Visit **joefontenot.info** and subscribe to the daily devotional. It's the same thought provoking bite-sized chunks, delivered to your inbox each morning.

LEARN
PRACTICAL
SPIRITUAL GROWTH

"When members of my church fight to start a healthy prayer life, I struggle to offer clear advice on getting started. Not anymore."
- JOSH TAYLOR

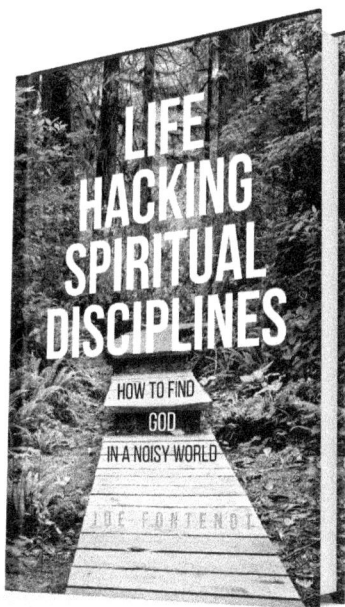

LEARN HOW TO BUILD THE HABITS BEHIND PRACTICAL SPIRITUAL GROWTH

GET IT ON AMAZON TODAY

www.ingramcontent.com/pod-product-compliance
Lightning Source LLC
Chambersburg PA
CBHW060016050426
42448CB00012B/2784